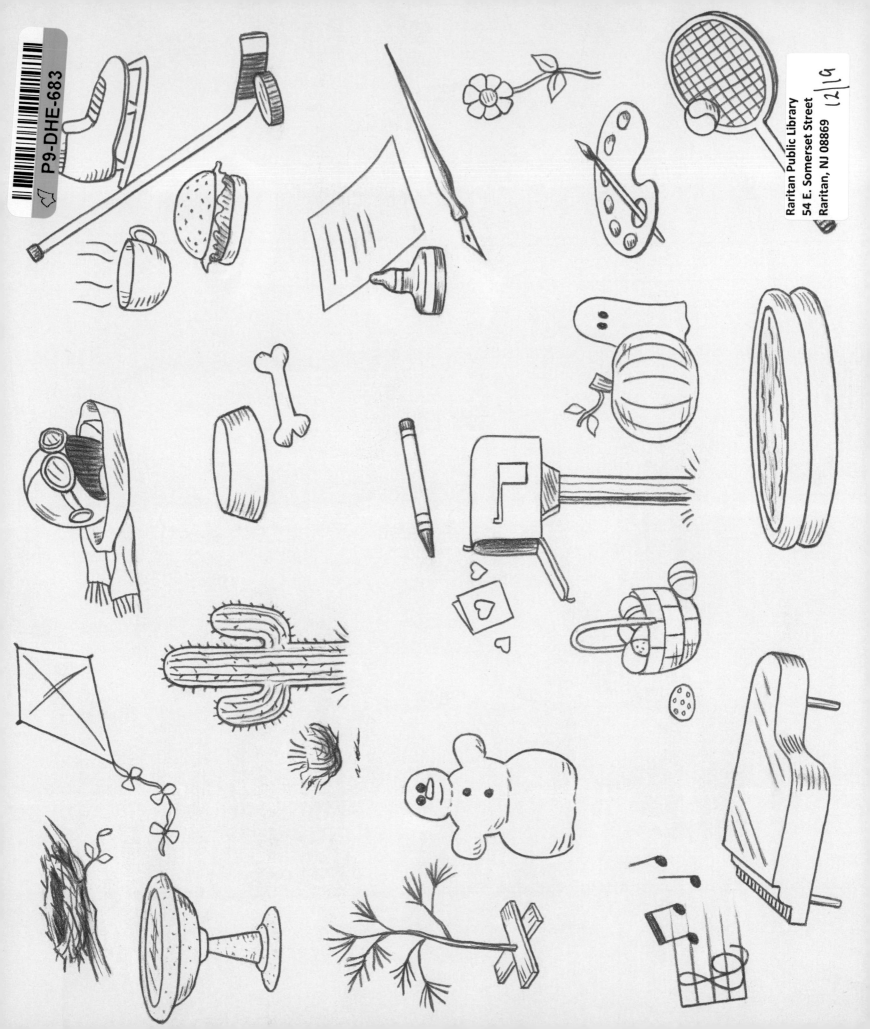

To Beverly Gherman, friend and fellow biographer
—G. W.

For Lewis, GOOD GRIEF!
—C. O.

Henry Holt and Company, *Publishers since 1866*
Henry Holt® is a registered trademark of Macmillan Publishing Group, LLC
120 Broadway, New York, NY 10271 • mackids.com

Text copyright © 2019 by Ginger Wadsworth
Illustrations copyright © 2019 by Craig Orback

All rights reserved.

Photograph of Charles Schulz on p. 34 © 1978 The Associated Press

Library of Congress Cataloging-in-Publication Data
Names: Wadsworth, Ginger, author. | Orback, Craig, illustrator.
Title: Born to draw comics : the story of Charles Schulz and the creation of
Peanuts / Ginger Wadsworth ; illustrated by Craig Orback.
Description: First edition. | New York : Henry Holt and Company, 2019. |
Audience: Ages 5–9. | "Christy Ottaviano books." | Includes bibliographical references.
Identifiers: LCCN 2019002894 | ISBN 9781250173737 (hardcover)
Subjects: LCSH: Schulz, Charles M. (Charles Monroe), 1922–2000—Juvenile
literature. | Cartoonists—United States—Biography—Juvenile literature. |
Schulz, Charles M. (Charles Monroe), 1922–2000. Peanuts—Juvenile literature.
Classification: LCC PN6727.S3 Z89 2019 | DDC 741.5/973 [B] —dc23
LC record available at https://lccn.loc.gov/2019002894

Our books may be purchased in bulk for promotional, educational, or business use.
Please contact your local bookseller or the Macmillan Corporate and Premium Sales Department at
(800) 221-7945 ext. 5442 or by email at MacmillanSpecialMarkets@macmillan.com.

First edition, 2019 / Designed by Patrick Collins
The art for this book was created with acrylic/gouache paint on hot press watercolor paper
along with pen and ink, colored pencil, and tweaks in Adobe Photoshop.
Printed in China by RR Donnelley Asia Printing Solutions Ltd., Dongguan City, Guangdong Province

1 3 5 7 9 10 8 6 4 2

BORN TO DRAW COMICS

The Story of **Charles Schulz** and the Creation of *Peanuts*

GINGER WADSWORTH

illustrated by
CRAIG ORBACK

Christy Ottaviano Books
Henry Holt and Company
New York

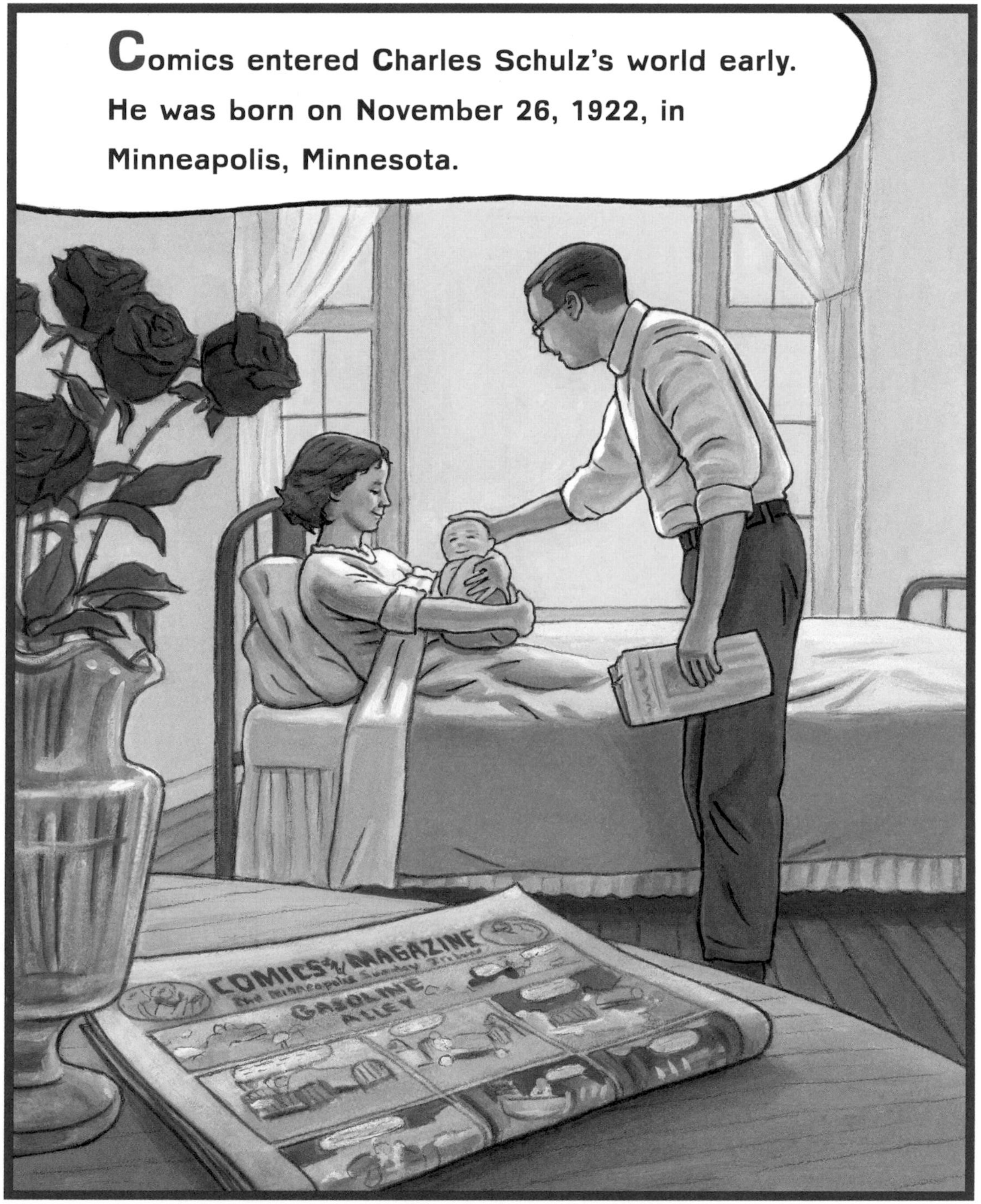
Comics entered Charles Schulz's world early. He was born on November 26, 1922, in Minneapolis, Minnesota.
GASOLINE ALLEY

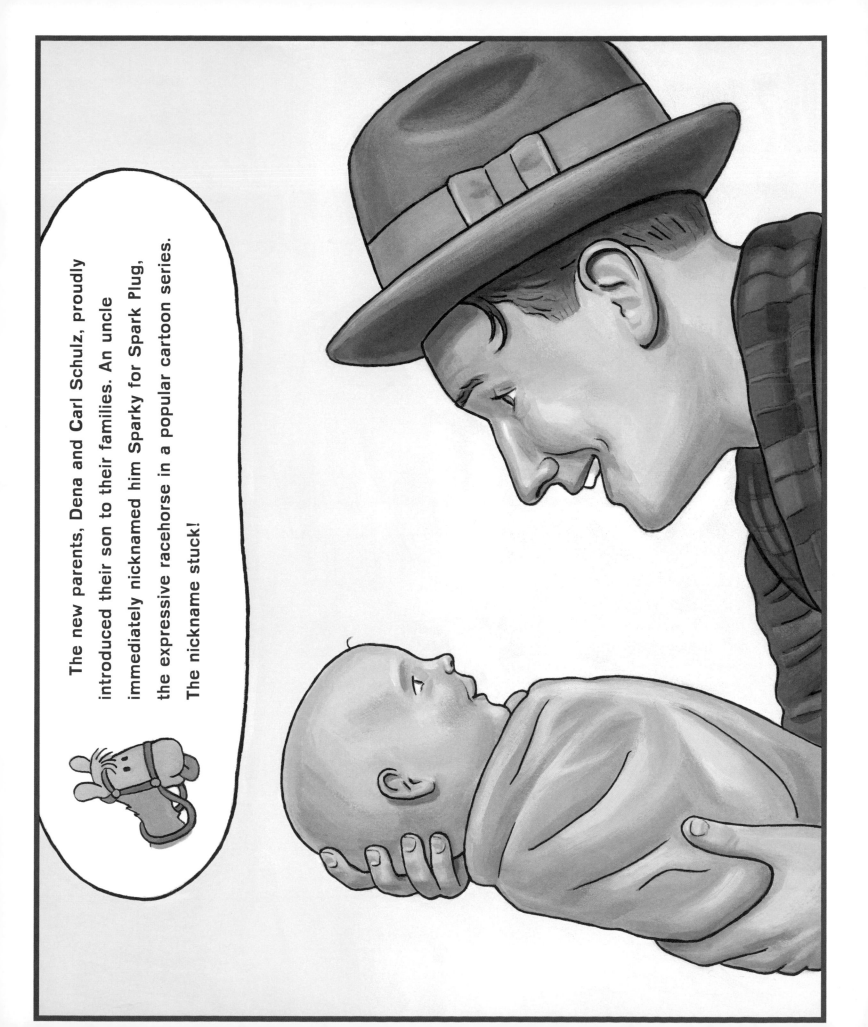

The new parents, Dena and Carl Schulz, proudly introduced their son to their families. An uncle immediately nicknamed him Sparky for Spark Plug, the expressive racehorse in a popular cartoon series. The nickname stuck!

Sparky's family moved from Minneapolis to its twin city,

St. Paul, when he was four.

One icy-cold morning, his mother walked him to his kindergarten classroom. He was daydreaming about cacti, palm trees, and swirling clouds of sand as he peeled off his mittens and coat. Dena Schulz had read Sparky a letter at breakfast from relatives who lived in the desert.

For art there were big sheets of paper and fat, waxy-smelling crayons. Sparky sketched a man shoveling snow off a sidewalk. Then he stuck a tall palm tree in a snowbank. His teacher loved the odd-looking picture. "Someday, Charles, you're going to be an artist!"

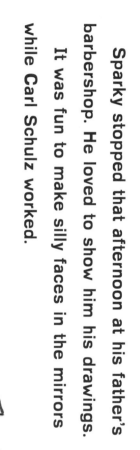

Sparky stopped that afternoon at his father's barbershop. He loved to show him his drawings. It was fun to make silly faces in the mirrors while **Carl Schulz** worked.

After the last man left, Sparky helped his father sweep the floor.

They stepped into the frigid night to hop a streetcar, and Sparky drew circles on the steamy window with his finger. Circles grew legs. Simple lines joined other lines to tell the story he imagined, until watery lines dripped through his picture.

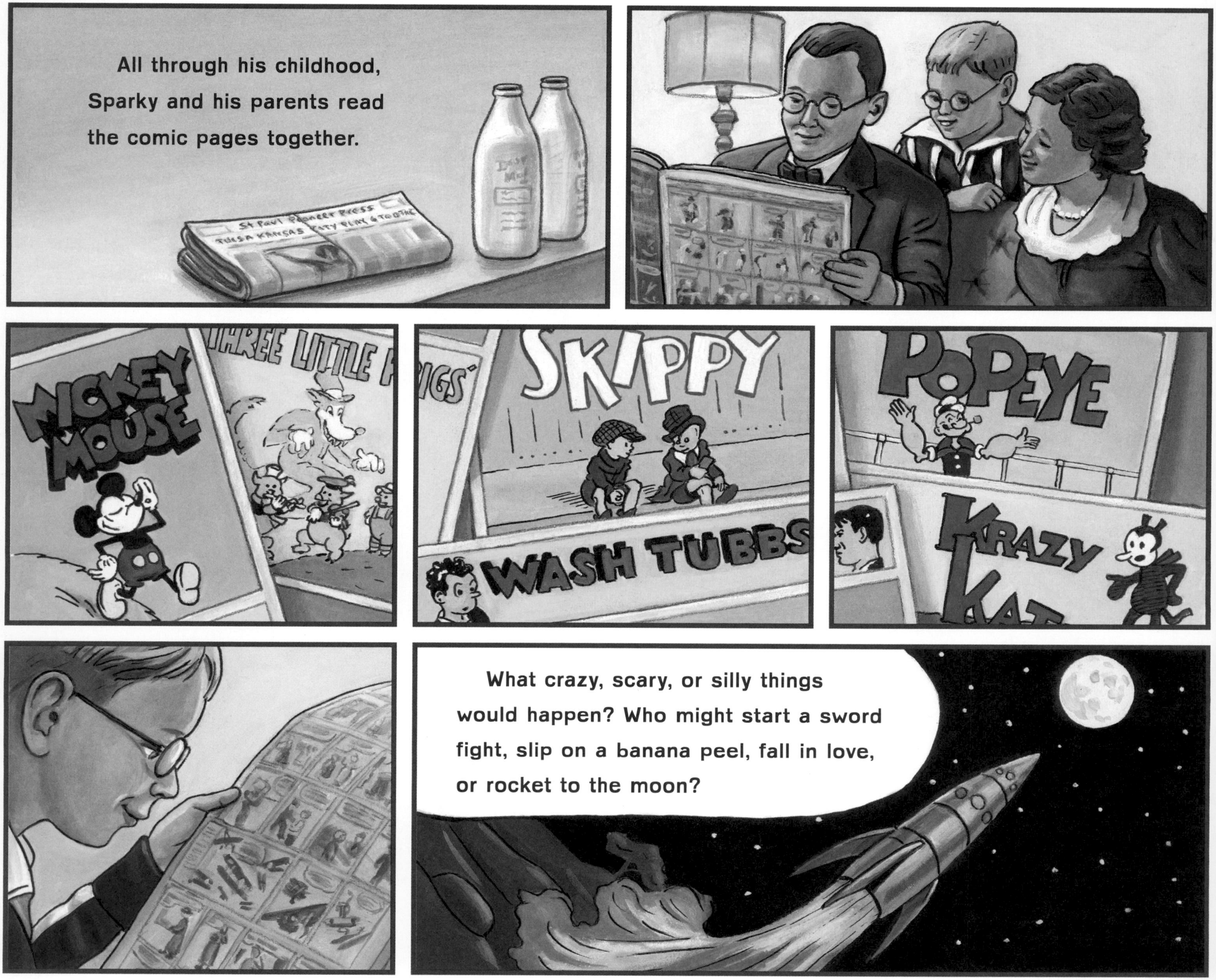
All through his childhood, Sparky and his parents read the comic pages together.
ST PAUL PIONEER PRESS
TULSA KANSAS CITY FLINT & TOOTHE
MICKEY MOUSE
THREE LITTLE PIGS
SKIPPY
WASH TUBBS
POPEYE
KRAZY KAT
What crazy, scary, or silly things would happen? Who might start a sword fight, slip on a banana peel, fall in love, or rocket to the moon?

Sparky copied his favorite characters on the back of his mother's crumpled shopping lists or the laundry cardboard from his father's starched shirts. Maybe he would become a famous cartoonist, too.

His drawings always made his mother smile.

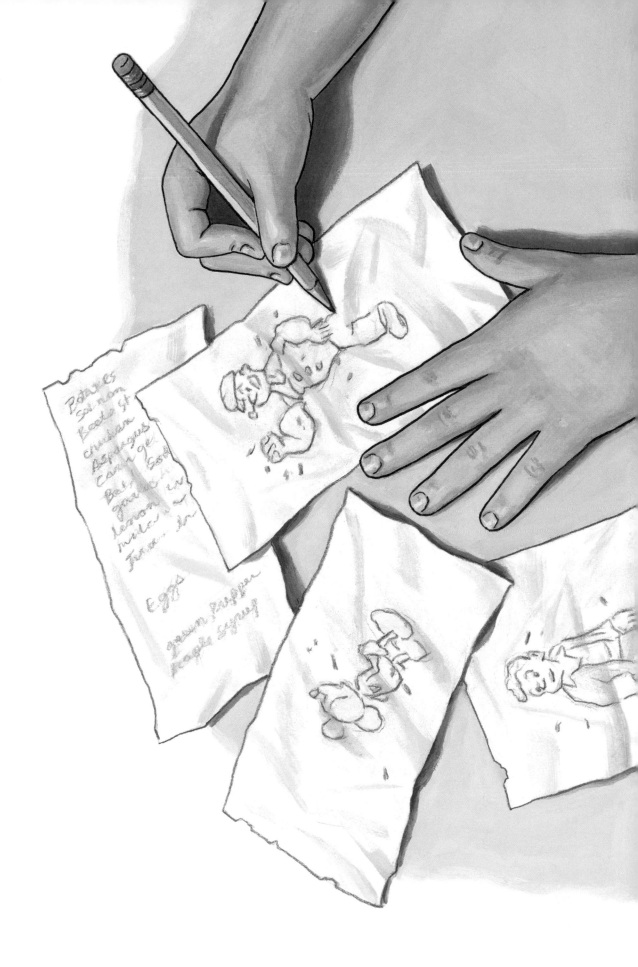

Every day he practiced his penmanship and eagerly read each poem, essay, and short story in the little blue books his first grade teacher provided. In second grade, Sparky earned a certificate for being an outstanding student.

Sparky continued to be a star student in the third grade, so the principal decided to advance him directly to fifth grade. Later he used his allowance and coupons from the newspaper to buy an encyclopedia at the local drugstore.

Sparky was also athletic and
loved sports. Each winter his dad
hosed down an area near their home.
The water froze overnight to form a small
ice rink. Sparky and the neighborhood kids
circled around the rink, raced over frozen
patches, or sped up and down icy sidewalks.

When Grandmother Sophia visited,
she played goalie by whacking away
the puck with her broom.

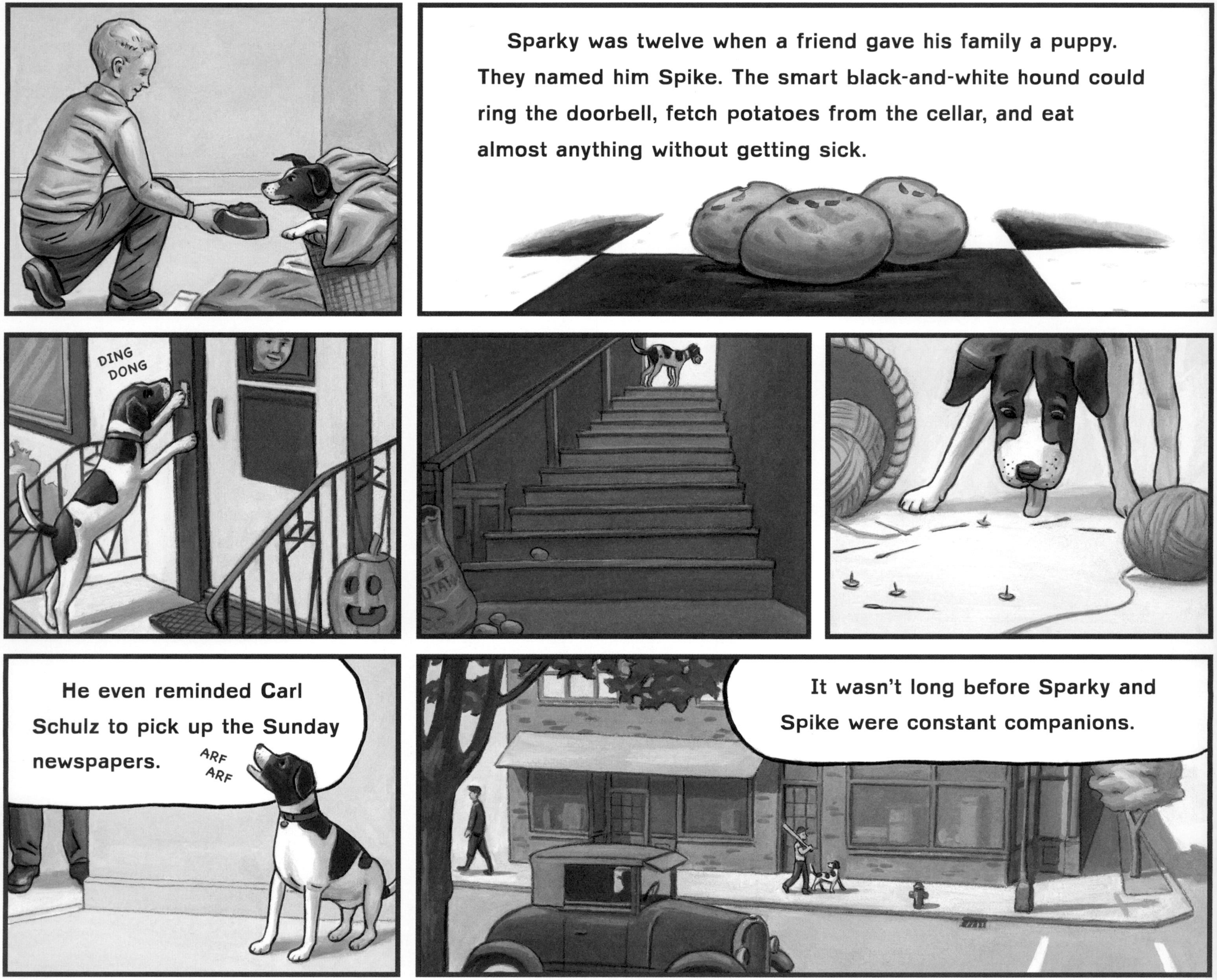
Sparky was twelve when a friend gave his family a puppy. They named him Spike. The smart black-and-white hound could ring the doorbell, fetch potatoes from the cellar, and eat almost anything without getting sick.
DING DONG
He even reminded Carl Schulz to pick up the Sunday newspapers.
ARF ARF
It wasn't long before Sparky and Spike were constant companions.

All spring and throughout the summer, they ran around outside until dinner. Sparky and his pals shot marbles and salvaged wood scraps to build hideouts.

The friends met at the park or on vacant lots to play baseball. They brought balls patched with black electrical tape, well-worn mitts, and cracked bats.

Sparky thought it was hilarious that Spike was quicker at retrieving balls than most of the players. The only problem—Spike didn't like to bring the balls back!

By seventh grade, Sparky was experiencing a change in attitude—he felt like a nobody . . . a short nobody in glasses who was surrounded by older kids. His brain switched off when he tried to do math problems. **Classmates giggled, and Sparky wished he were invisible.**

Each evening, Sparky headed to his bedroom. What should he do first—homework or drawing? Most nights he sketched comic book characters, Spike, or the neighborhood baseball games.

Knowing how much Sparky loved comics, his parents took him to an exhibit of comic strip art at St. Paul Public Library.

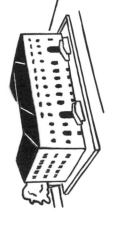

Sparky looked closely at each piece. Here were original works from the professionals' hands, complete with pen lines, dots of spilled ink, glue stains, and paper pasted over lettering to correct mistakes. Editors had written notes around the edges of many pictures, suggesting revisions. Even so, the professional artists were good! Very good!

After returning from the exhibit, Sparky ripped up *all* his drawings. He was determined to make his own work even better. He set out a pad of plain paper he had just purchased with his allowance.

While Sparky sharpened all his pencils, Spike snacked on shavings that fluttered to the floor. It would be easy to sketch Spike's naughty adventures.

One day, Sparky finished a new drawing of Spike.

He mailed it to Bob Ripley for his daily *Believe It or Not* cartoon, and it was printed in hundreds of newspapers.

Sparky and his buddies roared over the caption describing Spike as "a hunting dog that eats pins, tacks, screws and razor blades."

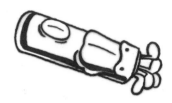

In high school, Sparky discovered golf. He joined his school's team and made new friends. To stay on the team, he needed to improve his grades. So Sparky worked hard and by senior year was earning all As and Bs. He graduated from Central High in 1940.

Some of his classmates headed to college; others joined the military. Becoming a professional cartoonist was still Sparky's dream. But how?

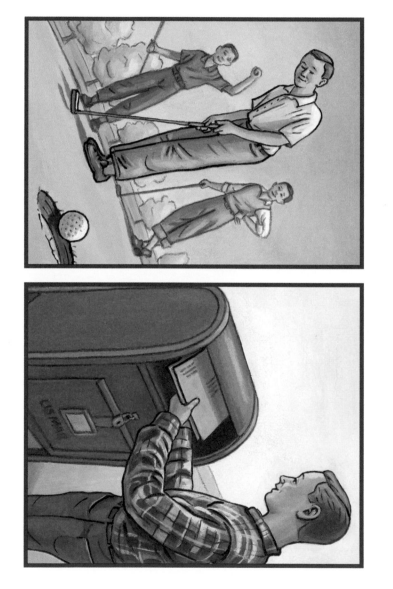

He cleared off his desk at home and started to draw.

Then he submitted some sketches to the *Saturday Evening Post*, *Collier's*, and other popular magazines of the day. He received only rejection letters.

His mother was ill and often in bed. He missed her laughter over his latest cartoons. At night she cried in pain. Once he overheard a relative use the word *cancer*, but no one talked to him about it.

Sparky listened to radio reports about a growing war in Europe. By the end of 1941, the United States had joined the fight.

A year later, the Army ordered Sparky to report to nearby Fort Snelling. He was assigned to an infantry company and prepared to ship out for basic training.

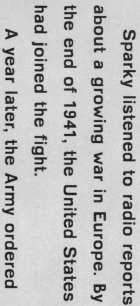

The last weekend of February 1943, Sparky got a pass to go home because his mother had grown weaker. As he was leaving to return to Fort Snelling on Sunday evening, his mother said goodbye and added, "We probably will never see each other again."

Dena Schulz died the next day.

After the funeral, Sparky rejoined his unit just as it was leaving Minnesota. Their train sped south, packed with scared young soldiers. It was only after he reached Camp Campbell, Kentucky, that Sparky buried his face in his bunk pillow and sobbed himself asleep—his mother was gone.

By the end of the war in Europe, a tall and muscular Sparky sailed home on a crowded troop ship. He dreamed of what he'd missed—his mom and his dad, movies, hamburgers, sodas, cars. Spike was an old, slow-moving dog by the time the two friends were reunited.

Sparky soon found several art-related jobs, but none creating cartoons.

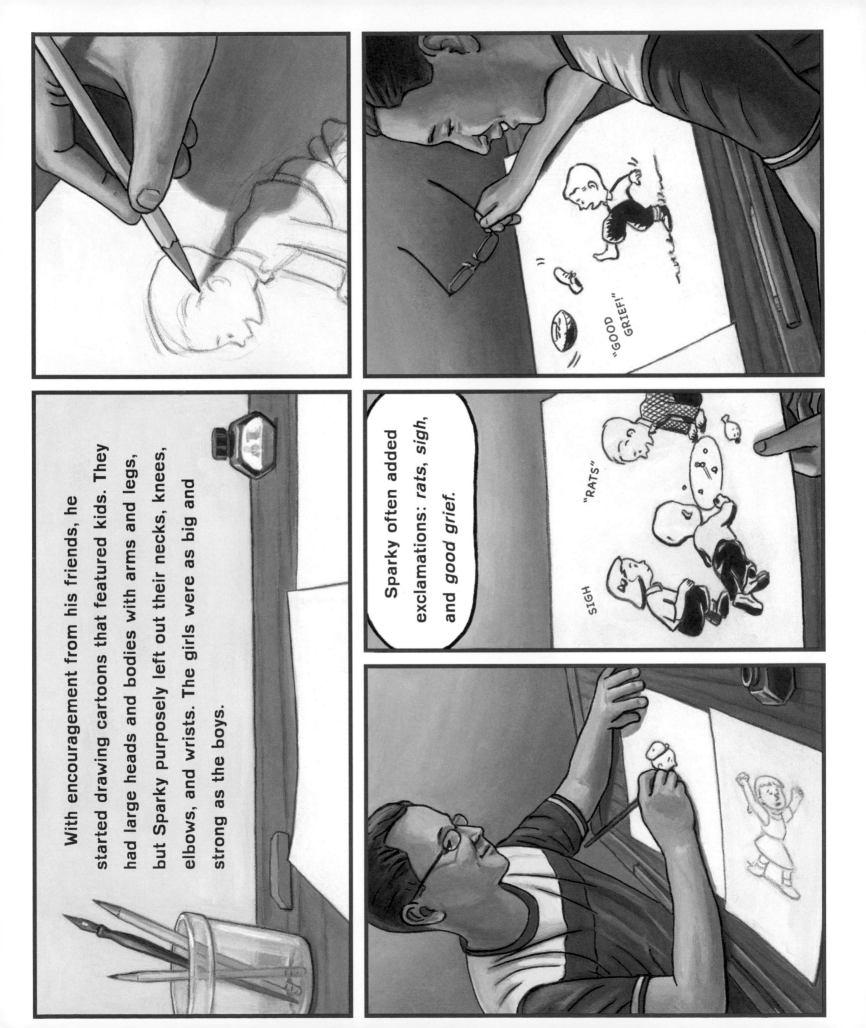

"GOOD GRIEF!"

"RATS"

SIGH

Sparky often added exclamations: *rats*, *sigh*, and *good grief.*

With encouragement from his friends, he started drawing cartoons that featured kids. They had large heads and bodies with arms and legs, but Sparky purposely left out their necks, knees, elbows, and wrists. The girls were as big and strong as the boys.

The *St. Paul Pioneer Press* agreed to publish Sparky's *Li'l Folks* cartoons. Sparky was happy to have the weekly feature, but the comic only appeared on the Sunday social page.

Unsatisfied, Sparky continued to submit his drawings to national magazines and newspaper syndicates.

Sparky sold a single-panel cartoon starring one of his kids to the *Saturday Evening Post*. He wrote a friend that it's "quite a thrill to get an acceptance from such an outfit." Eventually the magazine bought sixteen more, and Sparky was able to introduce several other little folks to a national audience.

One day he received a special letter inviting him to **New York City** to discuss syndicating *Li'l Folks* in newspapers all over the United States.

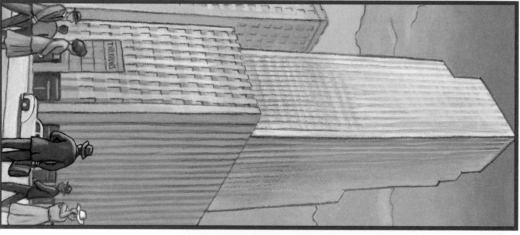

Sweating in his only suit, Sparky rode an elevator up a skyscraper.

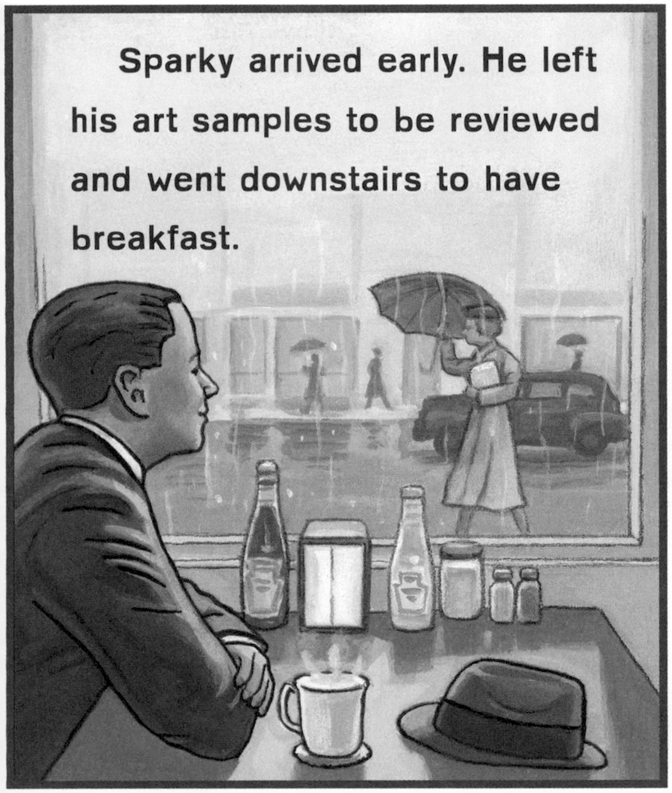
Sparky arrived early. He left his art samples to be reviewed and went downstairs to have breakfast.

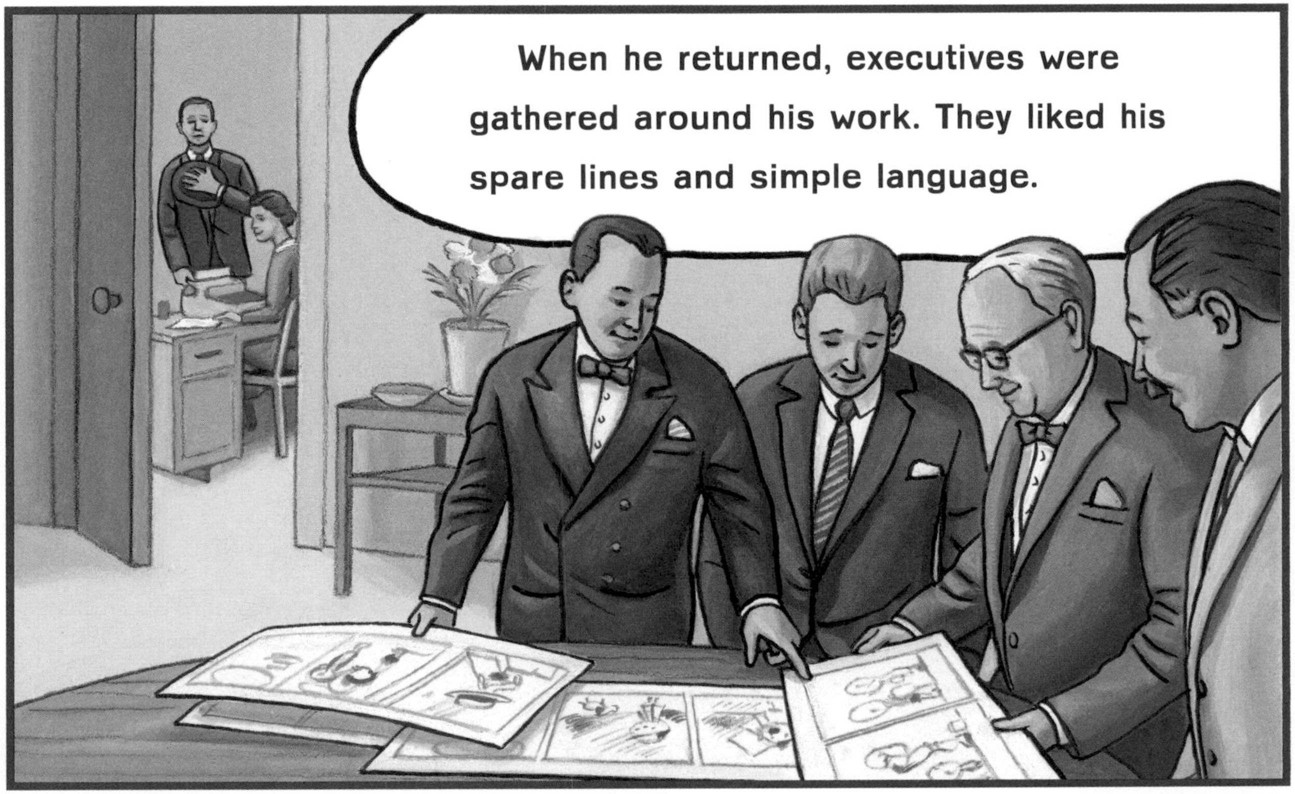
When he returned, executives were gathered around his work. They liked his spare lines and simple language.

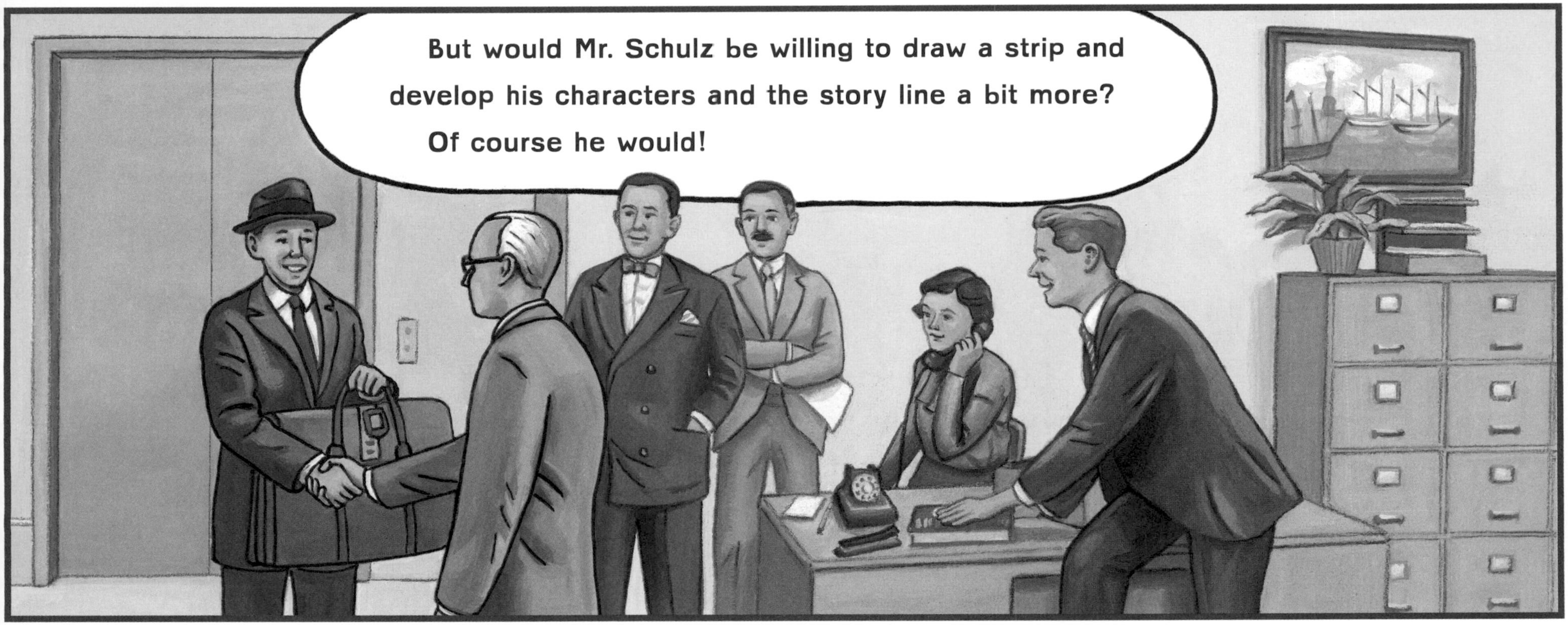
But would Mr. Schulz be willing to draw a strip and develop his characters and the story line a bit more? Of course he would!

Two days later, the United Feature Syndicate offered Sparky a five-year contract to market his daily comic strip to newspapers around the country. The syndicate renamed it *Peanuts.*

PEANUTS

by
CHARLES M. SCHULZ

On the train heading home, Sparky celebrated with a steak dinner. The kindergarten teacher who had admired Sparky's drawing of a palm tree sticking out of a snowbank was right. Sparky had never forgotten her words of praise. He was an artist and on his way in the world.

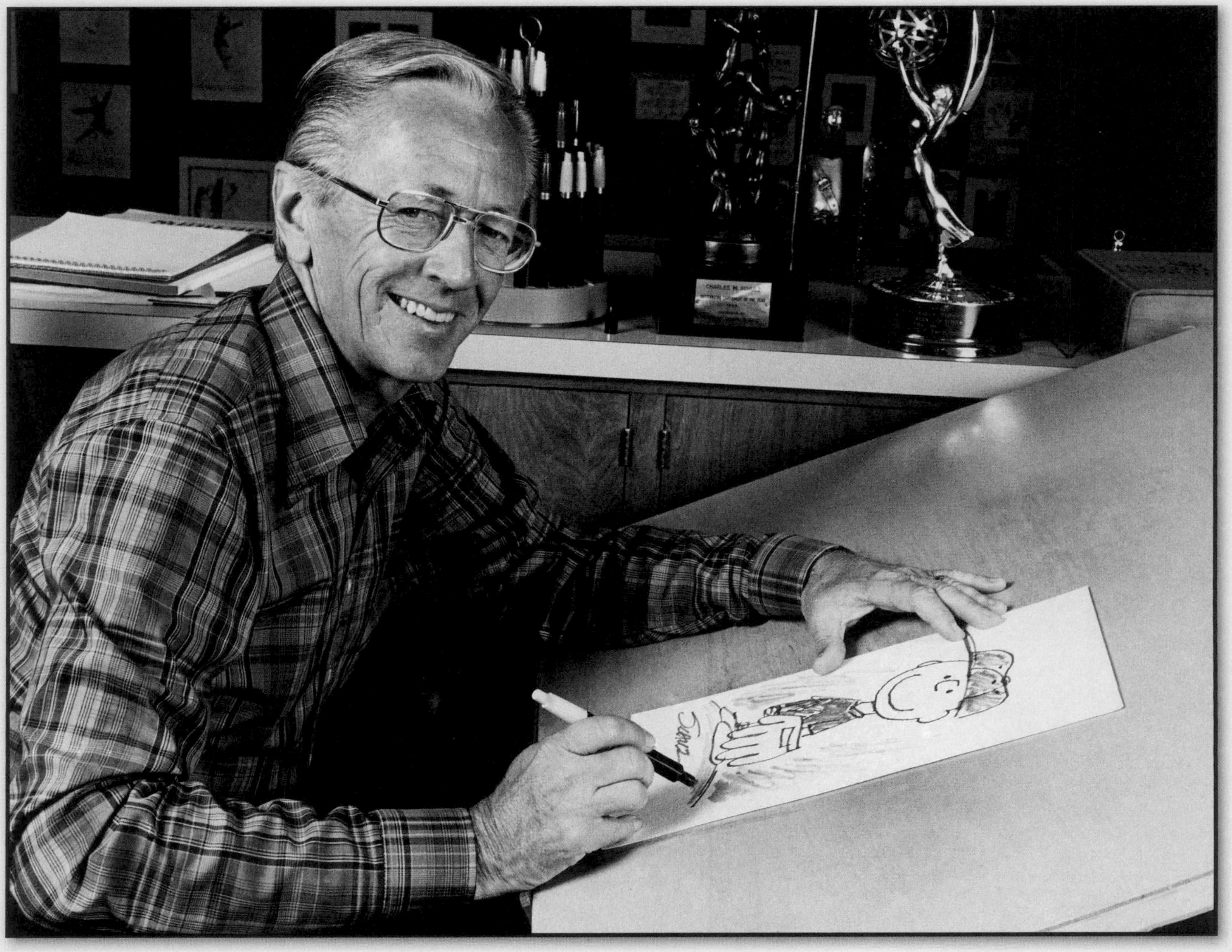

Charles Schulz—the artist at work

AUTHOR'S NOTE

CHARLES SCHULZ never liked the name *Peanuts* for his strip. He felt he was drawing kids, not something as insignificant as a circus snack. Seven newspapers published *Peanuts* in 1950. After five years, to his amazement, it ran in one hundred papers. Ten years later, *Peanuts* was among the country's most widely circulated comic strips, and the name had really caught on.

Sparky married Joyce Halverson in 1951. Tired of the long winters in Minnesota, they moved from Minneapolis to Sebastopol, California, in 1958. They built a house for themselves and their five children. But the marriage didn't last, and Sparky and Joyce divorced. In 1973, he married Jean Forsyth Clyde, and they moved to nearby Santa Rosa.

Each week Sparky completed six strips plus the longer Sunday comic in his studio, One Snoopy Place. He scribbled ideas on notepaper until he was pleased with his story. Then on art paper he carefully inked the lines for his characters and speech balloons. If the strip was to be printed in color, he chose the colors from a numbered chart. Color was added mechanically by each newspaper's printer.

He always made time to encourage aspiring cartoonists in person or by letter. Fan mail arrived daily, and Sparky tried to answer it all. He might tell a fan to practice drawing every day. He often suggested they study the shape of a person's arms or how muscles popped, doing what he called "mental drawing."

Art education was important to Sparky. His father had worked extra hours to pay for Sparky's correspondence course with the Federal School of Illustrating and Cartooning, later renamed Art Instruction, Inc. After the war, the school helped Sparky find a job lettering comics he didn't draw—every bit of training helped—and then hired him as a full-time instructor.

From 1950 until his death on February 12, 2000, at the age of seventy-seven, Charles "Sparky" Schulz completed 17,897 strips. By then, *Peanuts* was appearing in over 2,600 newspapers around the world. It was one of the longest-running illustrated comic series drawn by one artist.

Sparky often said that he was "born to draw comic strips." For fifty years he used simple lines and language to create the memorable *Peanuts* gang that continues to be discovered and loved by readers of all ages.

ARTIST'S NOTE

Much like Sparky, I learned to draw better as a child by copying my favorite cartoon characters—Charlie Brown and Snoopy. Charles Schulz's black-and-white line drawings appear simple, but they are harder to replicate than you might think. Just try it!

Rereading thousands of *Peanuts* strips was the most enjoyable "research" I've ever undertaken. If you are a *Peanuts* fan, keep an eye out in this book for references to his comics that I added to the art, like Snoopy's doghouse and red supper dish and Linus's blue blanket. I traveled to St. Paul, Minnesota, to explore and photograph Sparky's neighborhoods, schools, and homes, including the St. Paul Public Library, where he saw the comics art show that excited him as a child. Sparky's story of hard work, determination, and resilience in achieving one's dream is both admirable and inspiring.

Craig's childhood drawing of Charlie Brown and Snoopy

CHARLES SCHULZ AND HIS *PEANUTS* GANG

CHARLIE BROWN: The leader and pitcher on a struggling neighborhood baseball team. Whatever he does, Charlie Brown tries to succeed, no matter how many times he fails.

FRANKLIN: The first African American character in *Peanuts*. Franklin meets Charlie Brown at the beach and they chat about building sandcastles and playing baseball. Before long, Franklin joins the team.

LINUS: A philosopher like Sparky who carries a security blanket to calm his worries.

LITTLE RED-HAIRED GIRL: Charlie Brown's love interest. This nameless character was inspired by Sparky's first true love.

LUCY: Linus's crabby older sister, who torments Charlie Brown, gives advice for five cents, and has a crush on Schroeder.

MARCIE: Peppermint Patty's sidekick. Marcie calls her Sir.

PEPPERMINT PATTY: A freckled-faced girl who's great at baseball but not at school. Calls her crush, Charlie Brown, Chuck.

PIGPEN: A human magnet for dirt and dust.

SCHROEDER: Charlie Brown's friend who plays a toy piano and believes that Beethoven was the first president of the United States. Schroeder reflects Sparky's love of classical music.

SHERMY: Named for Sparky's boyhood friend, Sherman Plepler.

SNOOPY: Charlie Brown's beagle, a daydreaming daredevil and an avid ice hockey player who has many fantasy adventures.

SPIKE: Snoopy's brother who lives among the cacti and coyotes in Needles, California. He is named after Sparky's childhood dog.

WOODSTOCK: A yellow bird that sits on Snoopy's head and ice-skates in the dog's frozen water dish.

❖ ❖ ❖

Sparky created more than fifty *Peanuts* characters over the years. Some, like VIOLET and RERUN, turn up sporadically.

PLACES TO VISIT

◆ Santa Rosa, California—Statues of *Peanuts* characters dot the town where Sparky lived for nearly thirty years. Two are at the national headquarters of Canine Companions for Independence, on the Jean and Charles Schulz Campus. Sparky drew a Snoopy in the sidewalk cement there as well (cci.org).

◆ Charles M. Schulz Museum and Research Center, Santa Rosa, California (schulzmuseum.org).

◆ Knotts Berry Farm park, Buena Park, California—The park features *Peanuts*-themed events as well as rides and even a theater (knotts.com).

◆ Macy's Thanksgiving Day Parade, New York City—A gigantic *Peanuts* character balloon has appeared in every parade since Snoopy made his debut in 1968.

◆ Landmark Plaza and Rice Park, St. Paul, Minnesota—Bronze statues of the *Peanuts* gang hang out in Sparky's hometown.

◆ Snoopy Museum, Tokyo, Japan (snoopymuseum.tokyo/en/).

◆ Hollywood Walk of Fame, California—Both Sparky and Snoopy have stars at 7021 Hollywood Boulevard (walkoffame.com).

SOURCES

Gherman, Beverly. *Sparky: The Life and Art of Charles Schulz*. San Francisco: Chronicle Books, 2010.

Inge, M. Thomas, ed. *Charles M. Schulz Conversations*. Jackson: University Press of Mississippi, 2000.

Katz, Harry, ed. *Cartoon America: Comic Art in the Library of Congress*. New York: Abrams, 2006.

Kidd, Chip. *Only What's Necessary: Charles M. Schulz and the Art of Peanuts*. New York: Abrams Comicarts, 2015.

Marschall, Richard. *America's Great Comic-Strip Artists: From The Yellow Kid to Peanuts*. New York: Stewart, Tabori & Chang. 1997.

Michaelis, David. *Schulz and Peanuts: A Biography*. New York: HarperCollins, 2007.

Schulz, Charles M. *My Life with Charlie Brown*. Edited by M. Thomas Inge. Jackson: University Press of Mississippi, 2010.

NOTES

"Someday, Charles, you're going to be an artist": Schulz, *My Life*, p. 5.

"a hunting dog that eats pins, tacks, screws and razor blades": Bob Ripley, *Believe It or Not*, King Features Syndicate, Feb. 22, 1937.

"We probably will never see each other again": Charles M. Schulz, *Peanuts Jubilee: My Life and Art with Charlie Brown and Others*. New York: Holt, Rinehart and Winston, 1975.

"quite a thrill to get an acceptance from such an outfit": Charles M. Schulz to Frank Dieffenwierth, July 17, 1948, Frank Dieffenwierth Manuscript Collection, SC2003.002, Charles M. Schulz Museum and Research Center, Santa Rosa, CA.

"born to draw comic strips": Charles M. Schulz, *Charlie Brown, Snoopy and Me*. Garden City, NY: Doubleday, 1980.

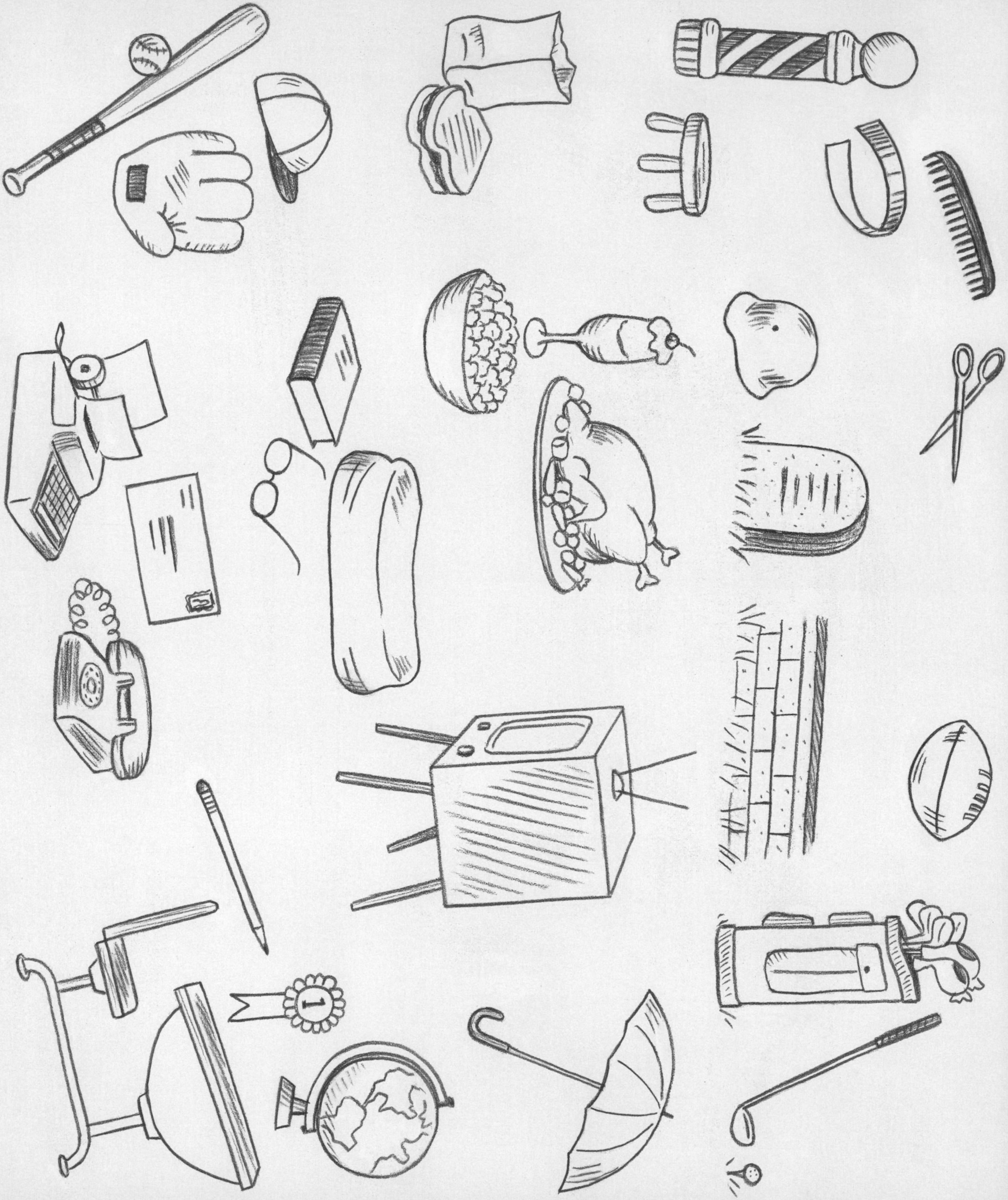
1